CROSSROADS
POEMS
ON
RACE
POLITICS
LIFE

ALPHONSO CRAWFORD

ISBN 978-0-935379-09-9

Published by New Life Educational Services
P.O. Box 96
Oak Lawn, Illinois 60454

Books are available from:
Amazon.com

Printed in the U.S. A.

Contents

CROSSROADS

One road is white
One road is black.
Intersection
Confrontation,
Conflict
Reparations.

One road is wrong,
One road is right.
Might is right
Is the gospel of the ages.
And the logic of today.
But is might really right.

One road is hate,
One road is love.
Intersection…
Bigotry seems to be immutable
Love is inscrutable
Prolonged pain.

Love is the only road…that crosses
The highway of peace;
Peace can also be a bridge,
To the road of freedom.
So many roads…Will there ever be—
Crossroads of Justice-Integrity?

BLACK POWER

Black power
Means more
Than being black,
It means
Do something…something creative
Build instead of burn.

Lets' get power through education.
Lets' get power from acquiring land.
Lets' get power from real estate.
Lets' get power from the vote.
Lets' get power as entrepreneurs.
Lets' get power from loving each other.

Lest I forget,
Lets' get power from God.
That's all we need.
To create something,
Out of nothing.

WE

We
The
People
That's how it started.
But
From
Constitutional
Principles
We've all departed.
Do
Not
Deny
A human life.
Please
Consider
Basic human rights.
Devaluing life
Promotes
Strife.

BECAUSE AMERICA FEARS

We came to America
Bound in chains,
Blood, sweat and tears.

Building America
And helping to maintain
Through the harrowing years.

Yet being denied
Equal opportunity
Because America fears.

Confirming affirmative action
Acquiescence to quotas
Repels listening ears.

There is no progress
Only time to regress,
Because America fears.

America fears
Her ethnic peers
Through the harrowing years.

WE MISS YOU

Dr. King we miss you
But your dream still lives,
With high aspirations…
Hope it gives.

Your dream was a real dream,
I now realize.
Reality can be changed,
We don't have to idealize.

A dream of a new world
Not merely a neighborhood,
A cosmopolitan community
Can be a brotherhood.

Times have changed
For the worse, for the better;
People are polarized
We're not together.

Recessions will not stop us.
It's bringing us together.
In unity, theres strength,
Strength for stormy weather.
We miss you Dr. King.

BLACK BEAUTY

Black beauty
Queen of queens
Mother of my children
Oh Ethiopian sister,
Your love has an aromatic scent.
That leads a native son like me.
From the distant shores of anxiety,
To the homeland of utopia.

Flower of Africa
Reward me with your perfume.
The sweltering heat of prejudice
Shall not destroy you.
I will nurture you
With the rain from my soul;
Saturate you with my intense cravings,
Blossom black bride of my passion.

Oh black beauty—my spare rib
Your presence is paradise.
Your eyes are the lights of reason
That project my vision.
Your lips are the wines of wisdom
I'm addicted too.
Between your breasts---
Are the depths of understanding,
Your body is knowledge,
I have known in detail.

EMANCIPATION OR REGULATION

Delicate decisions
Political expediency
Finally EMANCIPATION PROCLAMATION.

Emancipation or reality
Rigid regulation,
Equals no liberation.

If emancipation, why are we?

Economically shunned
Politically stunned,
Socially afflicted
Psychologically conflicted.

I'm tired of:
-oppressions
-recessions
-depressions

I'm tired of:
-Being the last hired,
-And the first fired.

Proclaiming emancipation
Doesn't make it so.
Action speaks louder than words.
We've got a long way to go.

INNER-VISION

I envision a world
Without suffering and scorn.
A world in which
Freemen are born.

A world without
Lingering oppression,
A world without
Blatant aggression.

It would simply be
A better place,
A world without
Obsession of race.

Where there exists
No more lies,
Where humanity
Never cries.

Where everyone receives
A slice of the pie.
Where love prevails
Justice never fails,
There exists radiant health.
With abundance of wealth.

RUN JESSE RUN

Run Jesse run
Amidst the corridors of power.
Baffle demagogues,
Flaunt audacious power.
This is
The black man's hour,
Bend the steeples of greed
With a brand new creed.

Run Jesse run
Run twice as fast,
Discuss domestic issues,
Our future and past.
Challenge them
To consider the poor,
Cause the poor
Pay more.
Will the needy
Always be forgotten?
Shall God's children
Always be downtrodden?
Will the expectations always perish
Of the poor?
Now that you're running
We can expect and get more.

We're standing tall
Stroking against the tide.
Is
Black pride.
Our dignity is intact,
Our self respect is back.
We can no longer be a shadow
Cause,
We're somebody.

From slaveships to championships
From disgrace to amazing grace,
Our time has come.
Run Jesse run,
We have already won.
With faith in God,
Look where He brought us from.
This is the black man's hour,
We've got people power,
Look where He brought us from.
Our time has come!
Our time has come!
Our time has come!

THEY SAY

They say that we're a passive people
But we know the truth,
Europeans are victims
Of enslavement too.

For they cannot transcend
Their mortal complex;
Decadent docility
No moral reflex.

No strength or power
To rise above,
An abominable system
With brotherly love.

To do justice to all
And live as brothers,
Or die as fools
With broken mothers..

They say….those people.
They say our communities are disorganized.
They say the black family is matriarchal.
They say the black man is a boy.
They say the black woman is a girl.
They say that we are genetically inferior.
They say that we can't learn.
They say that we are nothing.

Why do they need us?
Why do they say what they say?
To affirm themselves.
They say that they're everything
We're not.
Does it really matter
A whole lot.

I don't care what they say anymore
Cause,
I know
I know the truth,
I know my history
I know that no lie
Can live forever.

LIFE IS UNFINISHED BUSINESS

I go
I come,
I return daily
I'm not through.

I try hard
Even walk faster.
Spend more hours…
And yet—there's more
To be done.

I have more plans and schemes.
I Still accomplish so little,
I understand less—no more
But I do understand—yes I do,
Life is unfinished business.

LIFE'S STRAITS...

Life is:

Pain! Headaches and heartaches,
It's not what I expected.
Tortured with troubles
Misery reflected.

Problems abide
On the darkside of life.
Teary eyed and sad
It hurts so bad.

Damning up the damned
Like a river—overflowing.
Dark clouds and evil winds
Contrary forces are blowing.

Philosophers speculate
But we participate—reluctantly,
In life's straits.

RAINBOW COALITION

Most people are inhibited
But of our own volition,
We are totally involved
In the rainbow coalition.

A rainbow projects…
Bright and brilliant colors,
Our message reflects
And embraces all others.

We must not exclude any
Since there are many,
All people must participate
In the presidential race.

We fall on issues
That polarize and confound,
United we stand on hope
And common ground.

We must minimize our differences
And on things in common unite,
We must maximize our potential
And do what is right.

Turn, turn America around
Before its too late…participate.
In the presidential race.

LIFE RACE AND POLITICS

Life is a game that's hard to win.
A sprint to the end without a clue.
The punches just keep on coming
Rolling with them is what we do.

It's harder for some, of course
Depending on their background.
Some sink without trace; unnoticed
Cries of mercy: an unheard sound.

Then there are the lies: politicians
Telling us things are getting better
In the face of poverty for most
A knife to the throat from a debtor.

This game of life, race and politics.
The circle goes around and around.
It's all you can do to keep your sanity,
There are troubles and woes unbound.

And we let them sell us a lie,
The lie we want them to soapbox.
"They did this to themselves",
Our minds; deluded, by shock jocks.

THE AMERICAN NIGHTMARE

The American dream
Has become a nightmare.
Inflation is rampant,
Who really cares?

There is mounting unemployment
And the outsourcing of jobs.
Depression of spirits
And vibrant heart-throbs.

Impoverished people
Climbing stairs without hope.
Disillusioned with despair,
Drowning with dope.

Drugstores are on every corner
Advertising descriptions.
Selling out every day
A vast amount of prescriptions.

Politicians dance and spin questions
With amazing flair.
Babbling bubbles incessantly
Blowing hot air.
Ultimately trapped in their own snare.

TOGETHER WE STAND

Together we stand
On America's land.
Home of the brave
The former slave.
Land of the free
With opportunity.

Divided we fall
Fall in the brawl
Fall and bawl,
Fall into the abyss
Fall into oblivion.

Failing to accept God's provision
Falling out of grace,
Constantly promoting division
Over matters of race.
We simply regress
Circumventing progress.

Common in fact
Is our ancestral tie.
I must belabor that fact
This is not a lie.

Together we stand on America's land.
Land of the free with opportunity.

SELF ESTEEM

I often see me
Through others' eyes.
I often see relations
Through kinship ties.

Positive evaluations are important
To me.
Belonging, recognition, approval
I seek.

Acceptance and love…I need
Without reserve.
Dignity and respect
I really deserve.

Negative expectations..produce
A pygmallion effect.
Diminished self image
A nervous wreck.

I need to love and be loved
For mental health.
Emotional health is the…
Best kind of wealth.

ENCOUNTERS WITH SELF

Wish
I had time
To
Change my mind.

But
The fleeting moments
Flow
On like a river.

Tick…tock…tick…tock…tick…tock

What will I do?
What will I say?
What will I be?

I
Can't turn back
The
Chimes of time.
I
Guess
I'll just have to
Face
Myself.

SPECULATION

Why does spring come
After winter?
Why do tumultuous years
Never end?
Why do bumpy roads
Always bend?

If death is near,
Why does life prolong?
If people live to themselves
Why can't they belong?
If people have joy
Why does sorrow make them strong?

I'm going around
In circles.
I'm like the sea
Disturbed and distressed.
Viewing other facades
Seems so complexed.

Why am I influenced by others
Everyday?
Why am I retarded in life?
I'm late.
Is there greater knowledge…
Will I ever understand---perhaps one day.

FAITH OR FATE

Faith or fate,
Which will it be?
A life second rate
Or a life that's free.

Fate is negative
And fatalistic.
Faith is positive
And realistic.

Fate is bondage
With dim forecasts
Faith is freedom
With challenging tasks.

Faith says…I'll determine
My destiny.
Fate says I'll wait
And then see.

Fate says…
I can't see
Faith says
I believe.

GOD MADE ME BLACK

Dear God, you could have made me
The color of roses,
You could have painted my skin
With the sunshine,
Or picked a thousand different noses.
I could have donned a chameleon's skin,
Forever doomed to blend in,
But instead you shrouded me in darkness.

Many colors to choose from,
Even the regal purple or cerulean,
Yet you painted me the hue
Of dirty clothes and grimy toes,
The color of spent fire,
The black of night
Sticking out in a paler sea.

Why God, why me?
Thicker hair, thicker lips, and thicker hips,
My eyes could have been green like grass,
Blue of the sky and sea.
No, only darkness found by those who seethe.

God, you made me black.
People hate me because of my color,
Ugly foolish hearts.
You knew that people would forsake me.

Maybe you thought to choose a color,
I could rise above.
Perhaps a darker color,
Would bring a deeper love,
Not piercing fearful glares,
With fears that fits, uncomfortable,
Like a shrunken glove,
You cast a different kind of shadow,
God, you made me black!!!

CLASHING COLORS

Blacks and whites bleed the same.
In humanity's neighborhood.
Segregated by skin color,
In the sea of life.

Yet fighting for the causes,
The hatred never dissipates,
It simply hides
Always flaring up.

Involuntary judgments repeated,
Angry mobs forming
A preacher shouts to mend the ties,
Demanding respect on both sides,
But neither will give
Until they get.

Cast aside shallow differences,
Open hearts and look around.
The colors blend.
Mixing into different hues.
It's the ugly hatred in us.

Here is the reality!!!
White is snow and paper and lice.
Black is mud and chocolate and night.

For every good there is bad
For every wrong, there is right.
Cast off society's broken rules,
Reach for the light.

We stand together,
When we fight the same fights.
Together and not apart
All brothers,
Struggling behind the same grey lines.

COLOR BLIND

Are you really color blind,
Or are those tricks in your mind?
Colors always blend,
White folks always win.

Assorted colors are assimilated,
In melting pots.
Powers that be
Deal with subplots.

Blacks are second class citizens.
Blacks do not have access.
Acquiescing to social proscriptions
Stifles progress.

Embracing all colors
Enhances and enriches one's life.
Prejudice undermines
And promotes strife.

Do not be color blind.
Open your eyes.
Appreciate God's tapestry,
God's grand marquee.

CHILDREN OF GOD

Behold holy family, fathered by one
Related to faith, blood, and mercy,
Words of love and forgiveness,
All breathing the breath of our lord.
Voices united in one triumphant hymn,
Glory on high, we are the children of God.

Sharing communion
Filled with His Spirit.
God's will and love, never ending
As it was and ever shall be.

God is refuge and strength
We are weak, but He is strong.
A leader we can trust, for all ages,
Him the protective Father, us the
Blessed children of God.

His messengers preach the good news
Forgiveness for all,
His biggest sacrifice
Bred our greatest gift.

Our Father, creator of heaven and earth
Overflowing with love, every soul invited;
Red, yellow, black and white throughout
Every corner of the world.
People!!! We are the children of God!!!

DIRTY POLITICS

The candidate doubts his own words,
Encourages empty promises.
Ignoring tax reform and infrastructure,
Siphoning off funds for retirement.

People seeking leadership and greatness,
Demagogues who guard secret intentions.
Living in castles
Amassing power as voters try to survive.

Speeches full of hope,
Moving people to fight evil institutions.
Overcomplicated bills filled with pork,
Coded words to confuse common folk.

Codes failed to fill the void of honor,
A greedy crew promotes the greater good.
Where is justice?
When did pride and power become so cruel?

A road map of unity used to segregate,
The constitution ignored.
The populous cast as a fool.
Mother liberty is silent,
Crumbling in the bay.

Founding fathers ashamed as tyrants rule.
Democracy should have forced them out.

Elections bought and paid for,
Bankers stockpiling goods.
Blinded by the politicians' smoke.
Veterans degraded and dishonored.

It's the same dirty water,
Under the same old bridge.
All presidents play golf,
Managing crises.

BLACK LIVES MATTER

White people think,
That their lives are worth the most.
It shouldn't take another wildfire,
To see them all the same.
If a man wears a hood on a cold day,
And another man fears darkness,
Whose breath is the same.
That sparked the flame?

A yellow belly hides in shadows,
Observing the intimidating pale blue man,
Tearing and shaming a blackened woman,
It is the snipers saliva that has greased the wheel.
Cowards, hiding convictions in wounded salt.
Maybe black lives matter.
Black skin is authentic,
Unchanging, it is real.

The tales of inherent darkness are the myth.
Twisted lies spun to segregate.
Drawing lines on fictitious maps,
Fueling soldiers of genocide,
Fearing all that you are not.

Black people brought this nation's greatness
Black lips shared precious words,
Rhythms, and poems.
Black faces innovating to save white
And bloodied hearts.
Black arms fought with you side by side,
Black lives should matter,
When they defeated you.
As much as when they elated you.

31

Children full of bullet holes.
Murder is an ugly word.
Black shouldn't lose its hue,
Fading into a sea of white.
Shoulders shouldn't cower,
Wisdom shouldn't whisper,
Black wrists should paint billboards
Loud and proud.
After all, black lives matter.

ALL LIVES MATTER

Children fighting over prejudices taught,
Fathers fighting pride against the lot,
Mothers teaching silence,
Confrontation curbing manners,
But silence doesn't twist the failing plot.
Change is loud, change is messy.
Change takes chaos, eager words unrelenting.

Teenagers dressed in baggy pants
And hooded clothes,
Or straightened khakis and fastened buttons,
Warding off the bullet holes.
Undressed in alleyways,
Beaten for differences undone.
Tortured because we are different.
Unloved because they aren't the same.

No one should fear
The ones who claim to save.
No more lives lost to ignorance or greed.
Call it racism, police brutality,
Call it any orphan name.
The words tumbling down,
Sinking into the sidewalks cracked.
Shouting words that soar
Throughout humanity.
Shouting words that
Touch us all the same.

When each man is just a man,
Regardless of race, creed or skin.
When each life is a life worth living,
When color doesn't mark the difference,
Between a grimace and a grin.
When human means your freedom starts
At the same point mine begins.

If society refuses to turn a blind eye,
And injustice slinks back
Beneath the sheets where it belongs,
When history refuses to repeat,
And the melting pot boils over
The rainbow accepts every glorious hue.

BLACK IS BEAUTIFUL

All color
Compromising shade,
Paradox
Black is beautiful.

All dark
Total light,
Paradox
Black is beautiful.

All warmth
Complete cold,
Paradox
Black is beautiful.

All comfort
Whole fear,
Paradox
Black is beautiful.

Primary color
For all blends,
That's ironic
My friend.

Fear of the
Unknown,
Keeps us in the
End zone.

Reach out
Embrace God,
Yield
Touch His creation.

Colors enrich
An existential reality,
Loving our neighbors
Our hospitality.

Black is beautiful
Primary color
For all blends
Paradox
My friend.

MELTING POT

America the future
The grand United States
Formed in times of war and trial,
The consequence of traveler's mistakes.

From the East to the South
Dreamers come, dreamers go
To join a perfect union,
They cannot help but grow

The flavor ebbs and changes
With each new citizen,
No time the same, nor place unchanged
When one claims the role of American.

Gracious to the struggling
Opportunity for the rich
Proudly bearing red, white, and blue
Though yellow, brown, black too mix.

The melting pot, the salad bowl
Bloody wars and glory days,
Land of dreams and place of chance.
God bless the U.S.A.
God bless the melting pot.

America is not always beautiful
With unresolved conflict,
Plurality of desires
Not a perfect fit.

Diversity of dialogue
Causes flare-up
Heat-up is what we need,
Shake-up to shock us,
Shake us into
A perfect blend.

The shake-up changes the flavor,
With adversity.
Shake it down
With diversity.
We are who we are.
The melting pot.
God bless America.

CHICAGO

Windy city
A breeze through your bones,
Wool on your skin
Architecture unparalleled.

Trump tower
Sear's but not
Chicago Tribune
A tribute to the world.

Love the theater
Love the people,
See the slums
But hear the joy.

Artwork beautiful
Capture your attention,
Don't let it go
Plan another trip back.

Take the train
Run not to miss,
Construction noises
Chicago.

BOYCOTT

No, I will not
Only one thing for you,
Only boycott.

I cease all my trade.
I stop my cargo.
You will listen.

My love is not fair game
I am not a prize to be won,
But a good money can't buy.

Start up foreign relations
Wake up the board of affairs
Put down your pride.

Will you talk?
No, then only one thing
Only boycott.

AFRICA

Echoes surrounding across the desert,
Vibrating off steaming jungle leaves.
A thousand hands are clapping.
Synched with swiveled hips and barren feet.
Kinship burning, passion yearning,
For the Orient of Africa.

Culture calling twisted tongues,
Howling.
Singing, together in celebration, elation.
A diverse culture of twisted tones
Finding unity in
The first step of an obstracized journey,
The history of every man, woman, child,
Africa, ruling that arid stretch of equator.

Bleeding, diamonds stretching
Overworked fingertips,
Fingertips that work together
Coal and pillage gold.
Hands that know their value
Begins in motion sowing cocoa.
Arms that stretch across the continent,
Trading hunger for oil.
A conquest repeated but never tamed.
Africa and her wild, authentic mane.

Dirty stories whispered at the well,
Tortured souls selling one another
Out of poverty.
The past is transitioning to modern day.
Invigorating cities redefining society
Ghana, Cape Town, Accra, Nairobi
Different vibes in the relentless sun.

Distant, but close to heart.
The same blue skies and fearless plains.
Soaring mountains standing proud.
And crying, waterfalls weeping
For abandoned brethren.
Sandy beaches, swimming home
Across the sea
Mother Africa loving men by roots and trees.

IMMIGRATION

Babies born to parents filled with
Pride and dreams.
Broken plans to build a better life.
They hold stacks of paper
And tiptoe through the gate,
Where hope is stripped naked,
Shot with drugs and quarantined.
Advocates lead our orientation
To a foreign land.
Instructing what we can and won't.

A new home full of tests and confusion,
We were craftsmen once with the value
Others were doctors, scholars and lawyers.
Our children want safety and knowledge.
Studying with rose colored glasses.
Seeking peace and prosperity.

Seniors glare at us, the youngest implore,
The middle-aged resent.
We take the lowest jobs, washing dishes,
Harvesting apples, bailing hay.
They don't know our value.
They don't understand our twisted tongues.

They keep us segregated,
It's all for the best.
Divided and colored by culture.
Fear of stirring the boiling pot,
While hatred created a new kind of danger.

We fled from dictators,
Who smashed our doors and divided us
Expecting to find difference
Old problems replaced by new.
A steady wave of hopeful comrades
Trickle in.
Dreams are dripping down their sleeves.

FAMILY TIES

The family is a circle,
Not the sun or a snowball
More like a whirlpool or typhoon,
At times, its strength and devotion sit unseen,
But when it rains, it opens every vein.

Family is an aging oak tree,
Reaching towards the stars,
Relationships bind it
At times the wood may splinter,
But it never truly breaks.

Family are lights shining from heaven.
They aren't always present,
At times, the clouds muddle the view,
Or the daylight dims their effervescence.
But they are always present
And they always care.

Every family is different,
Members are playing different roles.
They may forsake you,
They may become tattered and torn,
Only family knows from whence you came.

Not every family is love and kindness,
Not all start with blood, though many do,
Sometimes their own members,
Other times a family will choose you.
But as they leave, one is always glad
For the memories they once knew.

Family is a hunk of land
Owned for generations.
It is the steady rock
At the edge of the bay.
It is something to come home to,
Something to belong to.
A place where you can be completely
Painfully, apologetically you.

FRIEND

A helping hand
A friendly smile,
Many favors
Last awhile.

Granting moral support
When you stand alone.
Standing with you
Whether you're…right or wrong.

Someone to talk to
When you're depressed.
Someone to console you
When you're in stress.

Empathy and understanding
Always there
Overburdened with grief
Someone to care…someone to share.

A friend gives:
-advice
-twice
-thrice

A friend is:
-funny
-money
-honey

A friend is:
-inspirational
-motivational
-sensational

A friend demonstrates:
-appreciation
-consideration
-adulation

A friend in need
Isn't necessarily…a friend in deed,
But a friend in deed
Is the kind of friend…we need.

SENIOR

You are young,
Yet you are old.
Your story
Is untold.

Feelings
You face,
Can regulate
Your pace.

If the truth
Be told,
You're not
Really old.

At times
Rejuvenated,
At times
Elated.

Did you know
Life begins at any age.
When you
Become a sage.

In
Your habitat,
You are
An autocrat.

Your wisdom
Appreciated
Your judgment
Mandated.

Senior,
Your age is
Well known,
Your strength
Has been shown.

10,000 meters
All is well,
On life's journey
You continue to excel

In your interactions,
Keep on forgiving.
You have given so much.
Keep on giving.
Imparting life,
Keep on living.

TRAVEL

Where are you going?
Here, there, everywhere
Start today.
Begin in Montclair.

Seven continents
In the world,
Bon voyage,
Ships on a whirl.

Across the oceans
And deep blue seas.
On a cruise with my wife
That's where I will be.

To Africa, we will go,
The second largest continent.
On a sightseeing safari
That is our intent.

There are forty eight countries
In Africa to tour
Nigeria, Ghana, Ethiopia, Tanzania, etc.
To experience God's grandeur.

We will also fly
The friendly skies.
Staying on course
Clockwise.

Constantly on planes
Like eagles we soar.
Constantly on planes
Hear the engines roar.

Africa spread forth,
Your wings.
A grandiose continent
Of queens and kings.

My wife and I
Travel on eagle's wings.
We have listened,
When the caged bird sings.

Oh Africa, you are blessed
Freedom rings.
We don't have to sing the
Lord's song in a strange land.
We can sing the songs of zion
In the motherland.

IT'S NOT TOO LATE

It's not too late
To make amends.
Take help from faith
Make time your friend.

It's not too soon
To cast sin aside,
Be willing to stand
Not to fall into pride.

It's not too slow
For urgent measures,
Pick up the pace
This is no time for leisure.

It's not too fast
For time to halt,
Strive lawfully
Be found without fault.

Time is currency
You cannot gain more,
By waiting for urgency
Or trading your soul.

MOVING FORWARD

I am determined to move forward.
I will do it.
All barriers are broken
With true grit.

In negative circumstances
I sat down.
Now I will arise.
I will rise from the ground.

Life has much to offer.
Opportunities are before us.
Life beckons us,
In God we trust.

I can't go forward,
Looking back.
I can't go forward
Entertaining flashbacks.

Now is the time
To rise and go.
Now is the time
To stride and flow.
In forward gear.

PREACHER

Vigorously, vibrantly he blows his horn,
For righteousness sake
Kingdom business is his priority,
Transformed souls he makes.

Repent for the Kingdom of Heaven,
Is at hand.
The preacher is God's representative,
God's holy ambassador.

The preacher is God's standard bearer;
In a world polluted by sin,
He has a message for a mess-age,
Not agreeing with current trends.

Crying loud against sinful social structures,
That violate God's will.
Crying loud against people
That exploit free will.

Constantly aiding in the uplifting
Of fallen humanity.
Spirituality is a vital component
Of Christianity.

In tension at times
Trapped between the peoples' will,
And God's will.
My what a chiller,
Culminating into a thriller.

Surmounting every obstacle
With God's love.
Overcoming by grace,
With strength from above
In a world that's in disarray,
The preacher relentlessly
Dispenses faith.

WORLDLY PEOPLE

Worldly people always,
Front different faces.
Worldly people are,
Always in different places.

Worldly people,
Sociable they are,
Worldly people,
Relational they are.

All are in great measure,
Obsessed with worldliness
Tremendously preoccupied,
With what they possess.

Keeping up with the Jones
They must compete,
Comparisons made continually,
On a clipsheet.

We all are stunned,
By each other's progress.
Shocked into reality;
Less we regress.

BABY

Small white bundle on the ground,
Not lost, but easily found.
With a yawn, the mouth goes round
In Hollywood, seven pounds.

It cannot walk, cannot stand
Its head fits within my hand.
The infant so small and grand
Bears around its wrist a hospital band.

Pick it up it will not cry
Tired of living it may sigh.
A small knee twitches and glazes over eye
Into dreams, the soul does fly.

Mom and dad take her home.
Watch her grow and learn and roam.
A life worth living, pure shalom
Baby girl a breathtaking poem.

Small black bundle on the ground
Lost beyond hope of being found
With no care, death comes round
In Compton, seven pounds.

CIRCLE

It all ends
From where it starts.
Essentially all people
Are an integral part.

The earth is a circle,
On it's axis it rotates.
Dictates and directions
Given by, God's mandates.

All of us are in
Circles---concentric,
That's why some are eccentric.
Some are egocentric.

We're constantly evolving and revolving
In different forms.
Straying from the path,
Straying from the norm.

In circles the world
Skips, dances and runs.
We all end up back
Where we started from.

PROJECT THY TRUTH

So does my heart throb.
For the wilderness heart.

So does my soul long
For the wilderness soul.

What will thou Divine,
Have me to do?
Is it to
Project thy truth?

With your eyes
I can see.
With your heart
I'll continue to weep,
For demons have conjured
Man's destiny.

CHANGE

You pick me up and ask where I'm going
I tell you the street and say
"anywhere here."
Neither of us knows the destination.

You come around sporadically
Sometimes whizzing around the corner.
Sometimes with warning
Neither of us knows which until later.

Each time I get in I feel a rush of wind
Closing the door locks it.
I've never been back once I've gone
Neither of us knows how to return.

You know me better than anyone
You're my best friend and my worst enemy.
Life is a nightmare
Neither of us knows when the dream will end.

I never feel regret when you leave
But sometimes I miss you once you're back.
It is what it is
Check out the tracks.

DIABOLICAL MIND

Obsessed with maliciousness
Promoting strife,
Thriving on hatred
Embittered with life.

Meditating on hell
Greed for gold,
Mammon is your god,
You sold your soul.

Demon possessed
Controlled by lust,
Proud and envious
Seek help, you must.

The physician is nigh
With His healing balm.
Your soul, will He ease.
Your mind, will He calm.

UNWELCOMED GUEST

The most unwelcomed guest,
Finally arrives.
Just a usual mission
Someone to surprise.

His appearance is shocking.
The company is left with sorrow.
Bid farewell,
Time you cannot borrow.

He ushers you into
A chamber of eternal damnation.
Unless you had accepted
The Master's salvation.

You're young with plenty of time,
Healthy with some wealth.
His shadow is near.
The messenger death.

REFLECTIONS OF TAINTED SIN

No man is an island, yet at times
Your spirit is disquieted within,
Isolation pains your soul
Reflections of tainted sin.

Insatiable desires that can't be quenched
Overwhelmed with burning sensations,
Efficacy of prevailing situations
Subdued by various temptations.

Bound to virtual weaknesses
Indefinite quest for relief.
Escape from reason through sensuality
Summons more grief.

Hell beckons you
Reflections of tainted sin,
The Master entreats you
With Him, New Life begins.

LOVE AND HATE

After a terrestrial transition
The world conceived.
Ghastly spirits of delusion
The innocent were deceived.

With a devastating explosion
The world was war torn.
All wrapped in bloody clothes
Hatred was born.

Love appeared and was tried
Innocent but yet denied.
"Save me"---the thief cried.
While Love was crucified.

Love is stronger than death.
It prevails over hate.
Hate enslaves and destroys,
Love alters your fate.

MYSTERIOUS WAYS

In the beginning was God
Creation phase.
God's purposes accomplished
Through mysterious ways.

Firmament composed
Stratospheric rays,
The Spirit moved deeply
In seven days.

Darkness and darkness
Finally, light was displayed,
Light appeared
Mysterious ways.

Search for the light,
God says.
Salvation is born
Mysterious ways.

WOMEN

Delivered unto the universe to shine,
Standing, shoulders back, restored in her glory,
The wonderful female.
Strong , fierce and a mighty oak—branches reaching,
Roots sinking down into the rich..crimson earth.
A spirit predestined to soar upward to the
Tallest peak of royal mountains.

Freefall down, deeper to the darkest depths
Of the turbulent ocean.
Running faster, fleeing with the sleek stealth
Of the enchantress gazelle.
Outrunning even the volcanic ash
And the meteor shower's stones.
Overcoming the agony of the rose's
Sharpest thorn.
Woman: the solar flare on the dark
And turbulent eve,
The regal queen, the tiny princess, a sphere.

The light to darkness. The diamond in
The sky of night.
Truth standing stark against a mouth of lies.
Lips and hips, prepared to redesign and procreate.
Soft womb from which to birth,
Comfort and become.
Minutes trickling by through the
Unveiling of warmth and life.
Authentic woman, clear and translucent.

Fluidity, melted from the frigid, snowy peaks,
Vulnerable and barefoot.
Tunneling painted toes into
Sharp and velvet grass.
Breathing in the sweetness of lavender
And lady slipper.
Shushed but never silenced,
Protected, never compromised.
Shunning insecurity fueled
By a poignant tongue.

Sway your hips, dance in the glory
Of the pregnant moon.
Surrender to your wild, ferocious femininity.
Step to your own rhythm, that soft familiar beat.
Listen, ear straining to hear the music
Of African tambourine and drum.
Sense the burning through your bones.
Radiate your love to man, to child, encircle
And enrich God's creation.

MEN

A sturdy figure bred by his matriarch,
Sewed by his patriarch.
Learned to rise above on the steam
Of his own beliefs,
Not diminished by another's creed or credence.
Trusting in his own morality.
Standards stringent without doubt or doubling.

A muscular man, educating his neighbor
And his spawn,
Teaching without beseeching.
Sharing the good word and his truth,
The mark of a good man.
Preserving family and valuables,
Carrying the torch when its weight grows heavy
Spewing light whenever he may journey.

Hefting the burden of his responsibility,
Demonstrating the art of manhood,
To his brother, father, uncle, nephew,
But most important, his son, his daughter,
The next in line,
His fearless legacy,
Evolving, redefining the measures of strength.
Upholding his land, protecting his clan.

Climbing the ladder so that he,
And others, can rise,
High above the trials of mortal tribulation.
A strong man, silent and humble.
Willing, ready, able to work
To create his own blessings.
Yet wise enough to accept the assistance
Of his Lord and his wife,
Holding the reins, leading the way,
Catching the fallen warrior.

A laborer, a leader, a lover, a provider,
The driver of the force.
Thy husband and thy father,
Taking stand upon the glory of the land.
Hailing surrender before disgrace.
Though he would not fall alone.
For shall he ever know,
His breath is the fire of this place.

FORTHCOMING BOOKS
BY THE AUTHOR

LIFE'S WAY UNTIL: POEMS ON FAITH/HOPE/SALVATION

TWO HEARTS: LOVE POEMS/LOVE LETTERS

100 WAYS FOR PEOPLE TO GET HEALED

100 SYMBOLS OF HEALTH AND HEALING

ADVANCED HEALING MANUAL

TRIUMPHANT/ 25 WAYS TO EXCEL IN LIFE

THE THREE GREATEST CHALLENGES OF LIFE

DOMINATE/ 25 DOMINION PRINCIPLES

WHY GOD MADE BLACK PEOPLE BLACK: 25 REASONS WHY

LEADERSHIP IN AN AGE OF CRISIS: 25 OBSERVATIONS

LEADERSHIP: 25 FACTS ABOUT LEADERS

LEADERSHIP: 25 PITFALLS/POWERTOOLS

LEADERSHIP: 25 TOUGH QUESTIONS/TOUGH ANSWERS

WISDOM PERSPECTIVES/ 25 INSIGHTS

WISDOM: 25 FACTS ABOUT WISDOM

GOD'S WILL: 25 WAYS TO KNOW GOD'S WILL FOR YOUR LIFE

POWER: 25 FACTS ABOUT POWER

WISDOM ILLUSTRATED

DREAMS: 25 FACTS ABOUT DREAMS

POWERS THAT WOMEN POSSESS

SPIRITUOTHERAPY: 25 PRINCIPLES

THE HEART: 25 FACTS ABOUT THE HEART

BLOOD: 25 FACTS ABOUT BLOOD

THE POWER OF BIG THINKING: 25 LAWS

MEN: 25 FACTS ABOUT MEN

PERSONALITY PROFILES: A BIBLICAL PERSPECTIVE

HEALTH AND HEALING QUIZ BOOK

ADVANCED INTERPERSONAL COMMUNICATION: 25 WAYS TO EXPRESS YOURSELF

FORTHCOMING BOOKS

BY ELEANOR CRAWFORD:

WOMEN IN MINISTRY: 25 WAYS TO IMPACT THE WORLD

WOMEN: 25 FACTS ABOUT WOMEN

WOMEN: 25 WOMEN THAT CHANGED HISTORY

WOMEN'S RESOURCES: 25 ASSETS

WOMEN OF DESTINY: 25 CHALLENGES

WOMEN OF WISDOM: 25 INSIGHTS

WOMEN'S MANUAL: 25 LIFE LESSONS

WOMEN'S WORKBOOK: 25 ACTIVITIES

WOMEN'S QUIZ BOOK

WOMEN'S DEVOTIONAL BOOK

WOMEN'S BOOK OF AFFIRMATIONS

WOMEN'S SERMONS: 25 SERMONS

WOMEN AND MEN: 25 CONTRASTS

FORTHCOMING BOOKS BY BYRON CRAWFORD:

SELL YOUR WAY TO SUCCESS: 25 WAYS TO SUCCEED IN LIFE:

SUCCESS IN LIFE: 25 STEPS TO THE TOP

LAWS OF SUCCESS: 25 PRINCIPLES

SUCCESS SECRETS: 25 INSIGHTS

SYNONYMS FOR SUCCESS: 25 CORRELATIONS

SUCCESS MANUAL: 25 LIFE LESSONS

SUCCESS WORKBOOK: 25 POWERFUL ACTIVITIES

SUCCESSFUL STRATEGIC PLANNING: 25 TACTICS

SUCCESS QUIZ BOOK

SUCCESS DEVOTIONAL BOOK

SUCCESS AFFIRMATION BOOK

SUCCESS SERMONS: 25 SUCCESS SERMONS

SIGN UP AND BE NOTIFIED FOR
SEMINARS/WORKSHOPS............
CONFERENCES:

NAME_____

ADDRESS_____

CITY_____

STATE_____ZIP CODE_____

PHONE NO._____

EMAIL ADDRESS_____

SEND TO:

NEW LIFE EDUCATIONAL SERVICES
P.O. BOX 96
OAK LAWN, ILLINOIS 60454

- HEALTH AND HEALING
- LEADERSHIP DEVELOPMENT
- DREAMS AND VISIONS
- HOW TO START A BUSINESS
- PERSONAL POWER
- GIFTS AND TALENTS
- RELATIONSHIPS
- PROBLEM SOLVING
- PERSONALITY PROFILES
- FIVEFOLD MINISTRY
- INTREPRETING THE TIMES: CURRENT TRENDS
- GOD'S WILL FOR YOUR LIFE
- STRATEGIC PLANNING
- ADVANCED STRATEGIC PLANNING: A BIBLICAL PERSPECTIVE
- MANAGING SELF
- MANAGING STRESS
- MANAGING CONFLICT
- ADVANCED INTERPERSONAL COMMUNICATION: A BIBLICAL PERSPECTIVE.
- HOW TO SELL YOURSELF
- THE DYNAMICS OF PURPOSE
- GLOBAL STEWARDSHIP
- LAWS OF POWER
- TEAM BUILDING
- ANNUAL WOMENS' CONFERENCE
- ANNUAL MENS' CONFERENCE
- NEGOTIATION SKILLS
- LIFE SKILLS
- HOW TO COUNSEL
- SELF MOTIVATION
- PEOPLE MOTIVATION
- SPIRITUAL EXERCISES
- NEEDS OF WOMEN AND MEN
- NEEDS OF CHILDREN

- NEEDS OF FAMILIES
- HOW TO START A CHRISTIAN SCHOOL
- HOW TO HOME SCHOOL
- BECOMING A CONSULTANT
- CREATING JOBS
- MARRIAGE RENEWAL
- SOCIAL SKILLS
- MOTIVATIONAL SPEAKING
- SETTING GOALS
- VISION
- TIME MANAGEMENT
- CHALLENGING CHALLENGES
- LAWS OF LIFE
- FEEDBACK
- SELF DECEPTION: HOW WE LIE TO OURSELVES EVERYDAY
- 100 YARD DASH VERSUS 20,000 METER RACE
- CHANGE AGENTS
- LIFE LONG LEARNING
- WEALTH IN YOU
- BIG THINKING POWER
- STRATEGIES FOR SUCCESS

ABOUT THE AUTHOR

Dr. Alphonso Crawford is an apostle of health and healing. Dr. Crawford is the president of New Life Educational Services. He pastors Cathedral Of Prayer with his wife. Dr. Crawford received his background in biblical studies from Moody Bible Institute. He holds the B.A. from DePaul University, the Master Of Divinity from McCormick Theological Seminary, the Doctor Of Ministry from Chicago Theological Seminary respectively at the University of Chicago

www.ingramcontent.com/pod-product-compliance
Lightning Source LLC
Chambersburg PA
CBHW060417050426
42449CB00009B/2007